Teaching Kids
About Money

A step-by-step guide for parents
who want more for their kids!

Helene Kempe
Nicole Clemow
www.moneytoolkits.com

SECOND EDITION

This publication is designed to provide accurate and authoritative information in regard to the subject matter covered. It is sold with the understanding that the authors are not engaged in rendering legal, accounting, or other professional service. If legal advice or other expert assistance is required, the services of a competent professional person should be sought.

- from a Declaration of Principles jointly adopted by a Committee of the American Bar Association and a Committee of Publishers

ACKNOWLEDGEMENTS

We would like to acknowledge all of the team who assisted in the production of the book including: Reine Clemow, David Nolan, Linda Kempe, Helen Bichel, Kerensa Little, Karen Alazas and Tinka Cowlam (cover design).

Cartoons were created and drawn by Sam Mackenzie - samikaze@gmail.com

We would also like to acknowledge all of the people who have contributed ideas and shared their stories.

Table of Contents

INTRODUCTION

Beware. I need you to know, and you may be surprised to realise, that you are already teaching your children, or the children around you about money through what you say and do every day.

If you don't talk to them about money and all they ever see is you taking it from an Automated Teller Machine (ATM) or the *hole in the wall*, is there any doubt that they will think you have an endless supply of money? If your children think that money comes from an ATM… you taught them that!

In a world of virtual money and internet banking, children rarely see parents sorting money into different piles for different purposes. Gone are the days of being paid in cash that is taken home for sorting into stacks to pay different bills. People have been receiving direct debits for their pay for many years now so the sooner you make money real for your children, the sooner they will have an understanding of the financial world and how it really works.

> . . . the sooner you make money real for your children, the sooner they will have an understanding of the financial world and how it really works.

Parents often wonder at what age they should begin to give children pocket money and responsibility around money. Some parents say that they don't want their children to worry about money and believe they should be allowed to have fun and stay kids for longer. Teaching them the value of money only takes a short time each week or two and can mean they can have much more fun for their whole lives once they master the financial IQ basics.

When your children start asking for Barbie, Billabong, Gucci, Prada, or some other big brand name, you know the advertising and marketing machines of the world have done their job! This is the time it becomes urgent that you help them understand the real value of money before they buy their first brand name anything…or more importantly before *you* buy it for them!

Designer clothes often cost four or more times the amount of chain store clothing lines and often go out of fashion in a season. The sooner you help your children earn the money to buy their own street wear, the sooner they will become more discerning and better appreciate the value of money. Marketing experts create a very strong desire for young people to buy to belong or to be in the 'in crowd' from an increasingly earlier age. Having your children really understand the value of money is the best line of defence against this pressure.

If you are in the habit of buying your children what they want, when they want it, you may be setting them up for bankruptcy soon after they leave home. There are very few first year salaries that can pay all of someone's living expenses and buy designer brand clothes and products.

After really thinking about this, some parents realise that they have tended to give their children everything they want so they can feel good themselves about being a great parent and a wonderful provider. If you want your kids to stay dependent on you because you don't want to lose your close connection with them, you may also be slowing down their growth into becoming a confident, successful and independent adult.

This book has been written to help you teach your kids the value of money so they can easily move towards financial freedom as they grow up. This open and shared approach to making and managing money can also help strengthen your relationship with your kids during their challenging period of transition into the adult world.

NOTES

1

KIDS LEARN ABOUT MONEY WITHOUT TRYING

Whatever you demonstrate to your children on a daily basis about how you manage and spend your money is giving them the opportunity either to choose to do what you do, or not. The period of development from birth to seven years old is referred to by psychologists as the *imprint period*. It is the period of their life that children copy what people do in the world around them without conscious awareness. The people they spend most of their time with are who they will most likely choose to copy i.e. their parents. The period of development from ages 7 to 14 is referred to as the modelling period during which children find role models either inside or outside the family selecting from parents, brothers, sisters, other relatives, friends of the family, etc.

Who did you spend most of your imprint and modelling periods (up to 14 years old) with? With whom did your spouse spend most of their imprint period?

Realising this modelling happened for you as a child, really important questions to ask and thoroughly consider include:

- What did you model from your parents (or significant adults in your life) about money?
- Which decisions did you make to purposefully NOT model things from them?
- Are you still modelling from them?
- How is that working for you?
- Did you choose new models along the way?
- How did your new models for financial management improve or hinder your financial situation?
- Which of your financial management habits and strategies are helping you move toward financial freedom and which are holding you back?

Whatever models you have chosen to use in the past, the great news is that it is up to you who you chose to model from this point forward. Choose the behaviours around money you want your children to see and do in their future. Just make sure you check in and see what results the people you choose as models are achieving for themselves before you consciously make the effort to start learning and doing what they do!

A great example of kids modelling adults comes from an interview we had with four year old Emily who loves to play shop with her grandma and mum.

While observing Emily playing with her grandma, Emily asked her how she would like to pay for her goods. "Will that be cash or card Grandma?" Emily asked. "Card thank you Emily," was her grandma's reply and gave her a debit card, which Emily then swiped in her "machine" to make the transaction.

Out of curiosity, we asked Emily where she thought the money came from when using a card.

"It comes from the hole in the wall," was Emily's reply.

NOTES

2

THE PERFECT AGE

Congratulations on being a parent who is prepared to accept the responsibility to teach your children the value of money. It doesn't matter what age your children currently are; now is the perfect time to help them. Ideally, as soon as you have made the decision to have a child you can set up the foundations for their financial security. The strategies in this chapter are for the parents to implement and manage, the rest of the book is about how you help your kids implement strategies for themselves.

The first step to establishing a good foundation is to open up two accounts for your child; an Education Account and a Wealth Account. Both of these accounts involve the funds being invested into long term assets which provide high returns. It's all about having your money working harder for you and taking advantage of compound interest - you don't need tons of money to create great results as long as you start early.

This is exactly what Nicole and her husband Reine did when they found out they were expecting their first child. They decided that they would open up a bank account (for his education) and an investment account that he can take over once he is old enough. As they were given more pre-loved clothes and toys for their son than he could use, rather than gifts for his day of birth, they asked their family to contribute money into one of these accounts to help invest in his future.

Whilst your child is very young, you are responsible for contributing to and managing these accounts. Once you are confident your child has demonstrated that they can manage these accounts and they are legally able to own the accounts, you can transfer the ownership to them. You should decide when this occurs based on the results you see your child achieving in earning and managing their other money.

In Nicole and Reine's situation, they anticipated commencing monthly contributions into both of their son's accounts as soon as he was born, with the expectation that once their son is earning his own money and understands what is happening, they will encourage him to also make regular contributions and eventually take over both accounts.

Once your children start earning their own income, teach them that a percentage of it should be deposited into this Education Account every time they are paid.

Education Account

Paying for your kids' education may well become the largest expense you commit to when raising your children, particularly given that the majority of young people choose to complete a tertiary education. The term *Education* includes both traditional education and also learning from other experts in business, finance and life skills.

To avoid your children having to pay a large debt at the end of their education, set this account up and regularly deposit money into it. Depositing as little as $5 every week can make a substantial difference to the amount of debt for education that may otherwise be incurred. If this seems to be too much of a stretch for your family budget right now, consider depositing some of the money given by family members and friends for your children's birthday or Christmas presents. Providing your children with the gift of having a debt free education can far outweigh the short-lived pleasure gained from receiving a new toy or gadget that they quickly out-grow, break, or tire of and cast aside.

Once your children start earning their own income, teach them that a percentage of it should be deposited into this Education Account every time they are paid. Your children will then be miles ahead with their financial IQ and enjoy the freedom of having little or no debt at the end of their formal education. This process also teaches them the habit of investing in themselves through lifelong learning and empowers them with the knowledge they require to reach their full potential!

Wealth Account - the Money Magnet

Parents can also achieve great results by setting up a Wealth Account for their children and depositing money on a regular basis using the same strategy as outlined for the Education Account. Using a Wealth Account utilizes the *pay-yourself-first* concept that the wealthy have followed for years. This means that no matter what happens, you are consistently making a monthly payment to the Wealth Account for investing the first priority.

The only difference between this account and the Education Account is that the funds accumulated can only be used for purchasing investments. All returns generated must be reinvested, allowing the funds to compound. The aim is for your child to accumulate enough assets to generate the amount they require to fund their lifestyle from the income generated through owning the investments.

We refer to the day they achieve this as *Financial Freedom Day* whereby one's lifestyle is funded by the income generated by the assets within this account and you no longer have to work. You are then able to choose if and when you work for money!

> We call this Wealth Account the Money Magnet Account as this is the account that will help your child reach their Financial Freedom Day in the long term because the money in it attracts more money like a magnet!

As your child grows older and is able to comprehend more complex concepts, start conversations with them around the benefit of having money working for you rather than you working for it; what compound interest is and investment options to take advantage of higher returns. Review this account with them at least each quarter, so they can see it growing for themselves.

If these concepts seem a little overwhelming at first, remember the more you learn, the more you learn and the best way to learn is to teach, so you will be amazed at how much you learn as you start to teach your kids the value of money.

Savings Accounts

Of course as your children's needs and (most likely) wants begin to increase; you then help them set up separate savings accounts to purchase larger items. This will teach them the importance of managing their money and to set goals for things they want.

These concepts are explained in detail and learned through using the MAGNET Money® system which is described later in the book. The MAGNET Money® system was designed for children aged 10 years or older. Go to www.moneytoolkits.com for further information.

> This will teach them the importance of managing their money and to set goals for things they want

Separate Accounts for Each Child

If you have more than one child, we recommend setting up separate accounts for each so that when the time is right, you can sign over the accounts to each of them to manage for the rest of their lives.

After all, they are always going to need money and will always be learning.

What investment options are available when setting up an Education and Wealth Account?

There are many different investment options available on the market to invest in which may seem daunting for most parents. Another important factor you have to consider is the tax implications of that investment as children and parents are taxed quite differently in Australia. Not only does it affects the net returns of the investment, by holding the investment under the wrong person's name (such as investing in the name of either parent), the income from the investment can adversely affect family tax payments, push them into a higher tax bracket, or hinder eligibility for the superannuation co-contribution, just to name a few implications. Therefore, it is important to seek advice from a qualified financial planner before making any of these decisions.

One investment vehicle often overlooked, which you may wish to discuss with your financial planner, is an Investment Bond. Referred to as tax-paid investments, these bonds in Australia are taxed at the corporate tax rate of 30% subject to being held for a minimum of 10 years and do not need to be reported on an investor's tax return. Therefore, if both parents are working and have a tax rate of 30% or higher, an investment bond would be quite an attractive option.

What if you simply can't afford it?

As at 1 July 2004, the government introduced the Baby Bonus to families following the birth (including stillborn babies) or adoption of a baby, in recognition to the extra costs incurred. This bonus is administered by the Australian Taxation Office and replaces the Maternity Allowance.

For the 2010/11 financial year, the total Baby Bonus amounts to $5,185 (which is indexed annually) and is paid over 13 equal fortnightly instalments for each child.

Certain criteria such as the Family Income Limit, apply to receive this bonus, so visit www.familyassist.gov.au or ring the Australian Government Family Assistance Office for further information to ascertain whether you are eligible.

If you do apply for this bonus, why not use a portion or the whole amount of this money to set up both accounts?

Every dollar you invest on behalf of your children whilst they are young, will make high end expenses such as education more affordable.

What about our own financial situation?

Finding out you're about to have an addition to your family brings joy and excitement. It may also lead you to start thinking about your own financial situation and ask yourself questions such as ...

- Will your budget stretch to cover all expenses if you take time off work?

- How much time off work are you entitled to? Do you want to take time off work? Can you afford to take time off?

- What government benefits will you be entitled to?

- How will this affect your family wealth creation plans?

- Now that you are responsible for someone other than yourself, what would happen if you couldn't work due to an accident, illness or even premature death?

These are all valid questions and important to answer. You see, most people spend more time planning a weekend away than they do looking after the most important aspects of their finances. A professional financial planner will be able to work with you, and in less than a few hours will be able to give you a plan and direction.

Think about this, if you were planning a trip to Paris, don't you think if you had an expert guide who had lived in Paris for many years that they would be able to help you get the most out of your trip? Well a professional financial planner will save you time, help you understand the complexities of the current legislation and assist you to put in place the most important things for you and your family. An initial appointment is usually complementary and will last for less than two hours. Wouldn't this be a great investment of your time?

NOTES

3

WHY KIDS DON'T LEARN ABOUT MAKING MONEY AT SCHOOL

Parents often ask "How come we weren't taught all the good stuff about money when we went to school...and...how come our kids aren't taught about money at school now?"

In fact, kids are taught about money at school. They are taught what it looks like, how to add it up and how to work out percentages. Some kids, if they choose the right subjects as they grow older, can have the opportunity to learn how the government wants them to manage their money to meet legal and taxation requirements.

> **What's missing and what they would really benefit from being taught is how to MAKE it and VALUE it so they invest and manage it wisely in order to become independently wealthy!**

The reality is that the vast majority of teachers are in the profession because they love to teach, help people and are passionate about learning. They certainly don't do it for the money – most of them are paid quite poorly when you consider the complexity and responsibility within their role as teachers of the most precious people on the planet – our children. Great teachers who are out to make a difference in children's lives rarely have an entrepreneurial mindset.

Very few are likely to be able to model and teach how to become an entrepreneur and/or how to make money work for you through investing in assets that generate income. Most of them never learnt it themselves and don't have it on their radar as being important. They are more likely to teach what they model themselves – study hard, go to college and get a secure, well paid job.

This became evident to us when we presented, at a high school in South East Queensland, to teach the students about money management and financial freedom. Their business teacher who had been teaching Business curriculum for over 25 years, also sat in on the class. The following morning she contacted us very excited, because she went home that night and redid her budget using what she had learnt and realised that she had the choice as to whether to keep working in a job until retirement, or whether to plan for financial freedom and take control of her financial situation. Whilst she had been using a budget every

year and keeping her finances in order, she didn't fully understand the concept of true financial freedom. She then remained focussed on increasing her financial IQ and a little over a year later she chose to leave her job and is now working in her own business feeling empowered and excited about working towards her Financial Freedom Day.

Prior to the industrial age, children spent most of their time with their parents. Their parents taught them everything they knew including what was important to them (their values) and work skills. With the onset of the industrial age, children started spending more and more time at school and less time with their parents. The school curriculum primarily focussed on teaching work skills to help children secure a job. Education about values was rarely included in the curriculum. As consumerism took over and parents decided that they both needed to work to buy all of the things they wanted, they spent even less time with their children to discuss values and day to day living skills such as money management.

Parents were now expecting the education system to teach the real life skills however...

The classroom environment at most schools is very different to real life situations where you work for and deal with money for real. It is virtually impossible for school teachers to make learning about money really meaningful for students when at best they can only use play money and simulated situations in the classroom.

The one example where real money may be used in schools is in school banking. Some clever banks managed to implement school banking into some schools – it proved to be a great way for them to have parents open more accounts. Parents were encouraged to send a small amount of money to school with their children to bank on a weekly basis. This was supposed to help children develop the good habit of saving money. Given the amount of effort it takes the parents to remember to organise to have the cash and send it to school with their children on the right day in the right envelope ... we believe it actually taught many children that money comes from mum and dad and that it is their job to remember to give it to you!

School banking can definitely be used as an effective strategy to help kids learn to save but only if you help your children understand exactly what they are saving for and what a benefit it will be for them in the future. They need to see the money they bank as their own before they take it to school. They need to feel they are banking their own money for their own reasons. How to do this is will become clear as you read the following chapters.

Ask yourself "When did I get real about money?" ... Most people answer that money only really affected them when they didn't have enough. One of the main pain points, many people experience is when they discover that they don't have enough money to live away from home...the point where being cash poor severely limits the independence they crave. Once they experienced a painful enough event in their life, they decided to learn how to make money for themselves and to later work out how to increase the amount they made.

One guy we know had been working as an apprentice for several years and was asked to go to dinner one night. When he checked how much money he had, he realised he would have to go to the jar he kept his small change in to be able to buy the meal. He told us that it was at that point he decided that he would never put himself in the position of paying for a meal with small change ever again in his life. He got very determined to learn what he needed to know about money – both making it and managing it! A few years later he went into business for himself and built up a very successful company. He then chose his Financial Freedom Day well ahead of the pack and left the company as a multimillionaire!

For most people, once it became about real money and real purchases and real work and real independence, they *really* started to learn. The problem for many is that they only started to learn…and once they had their mortgage and a steady job, they remained in an almost trancelike situation of going to work to pay the bills. They forgot to continue to learn more about money in order to keep improving their financial situation. In what seemed like no time at all, the kids grew up, went to college and left home.

The parents were so busy working and running manic activities schedules for the children, they didn't even notice they weren't making the time to learn about how to really get their money working for them. It was all perfect though, because raising their children was the most important thing in their lives. They just forgot to step back and realise that by spending some regular and dedicated time on learning about money, they could have saved a great deal of time in the long term and also earned them a great deal more money than just working their day jobs.

Parents **didn't learn to be** entrepreneurs when **they went to school and it would be** highly unlikely that schools would train their teachers to be entrepreneurs today either. When will now be the perfect time to take the bull by the horns and make your children's learning about money real for them at home?

As parents you have the perfect opportunity to help your children learn about money from an early age. Preferably early enough that they learn really good habits around wealth creation and not even notice they are learning. Good modelling and habits as part of your family life are amazingly powerful tools for success.

Committing some time and effort in the short term will save you and your kids in many, many ways in the long term...and everyone gets to win and have a better life! So what are you waiting for?...let's get started!

4

MAKE IT REAL FOR THEM

Parents have the perfect opportunity to help their children learn about money at the age that suits them perfectly. At school a child's learning is dictated by the government. The curriculum teachers are required to teach is forced into age level programs to cater for the need to assess students' progress. The problem with this is that children develop at their own pace irrespective of the school system.

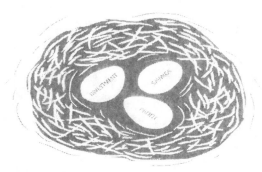

One mother we interviewed mentioned that her son went to watch the stock market floor in action when he was nine years old, at his request. He had watched a television program and got hooked on the concept, started reading about it on the Internet and then kept asking to go until his dad organised a visit to the viewing room. He was then inspired to start saving money for his first investment share portfolio.

We have no doubt that parents have the best real life opportunity to put learning about money into practice. You can do it easily by making it part of family life through how you introduce and manage giving your children an allowance or pocket money. You have an amazing opportunity to make their learning highly effective through showing them how to earn additional money by being paid for certain tasks they do around the home.

We all learn once we have enough reason to. How many couples do you know who suddenly had to get very real about making and managing money when they fell pregnant? They had their finances comfortable enough for two and then had to rethink and rework their finances to include their child. Keeping children safe and secure is one of the strongest drivers for parents to make money. This driver can be so strong in fact that many parents have enough *skin in the game* to stay in jobs they hate for years in order to pay the bills and provide for their children.

Once you have a really good reason to make money i.e. once you have enough skin in the game, you then become really aware of what you are doing until you work out how to make enough money to keep you and your family safe and secure. When people focus on their financial situation in times of need, they often work out how to fix it in the short term and once they feel safe with it; they just do the same thing over and over until the next strong need presents itself. How much better would it be to keep increasing your financial IQ and therefore your wealth so that all of your needs are planned for and met in advance?

Developing effective money habits is critical to being able to keep money as a resource that is exchanged to get what you want. How much easier would it have been if you had developed resourceful money habits *before you even knew you were learning them?*

Ensuring that earning and managing money becomes an everyday part of your children's lives as soon as they can grasp the basic concepts can take stress about money out of their lives. Helping them develop financial IQ at an early age so they will be financially secure in the future will no doubt also give you peace of mind.

> Developing effective money habits is critical to being able to keep money as a resource that is exchanged to get what you want.

NOTES

5

KIDS DO AS YOU DO,
NOT AS YOU SAY!

...ever **heard** parents say "If I have told you once,
I have told you a **thousand times.** Why don't you ...?"

I f you remember those or similar words coming out of your parents' mouths, then there is a very good chance similar words have come from your mouth when asking your children to do something around the house, or perhaps their homework.

No one likes to be told what to do – think about it, do you? So why do we waste so much breath telling children what to do? Children learn by watching what you do and then deciding whether to do it themselves or not. If they like what they see, they will want to know more and ask you questions so they can learn to do it for themselves. If they don't like what they see (maybe it looks like hard work or is too messy) they will not do what you do and will resist your attempts.

The only way to make someone do something they would rather not do is to make the reward worth the effort. This can be done in two ways. Either we offer 'payment' e.g. "Once you have done your homework you can go and play." Or we give them the pain they will get if they don't do it e.g. "If you don't clean up your room, I will take your toys away." Take a few minutes to consider how you convince your children to do things they don't want to do. We all do everything to either get something we perceive as 'good' or avoid something we think of as 'bad'.

> The only way to make someone do something they would rather not do is to make the reward worth the effort.

What jobs can you think of that you have chosen to do even though you hate doing them? What was your reward for choosing to do those jobs? It may have been the money to feed your children (one of the most powerful motivators on the planet) or the payment for an air ticket to go on a holiday. It may have been that you really wanted to help someone in need. Whatever the reason, remember you chose to do it. No-one can physically push your limbs around repeatedly to make you do anything. At some point for whatever reason, you make the decision to do any task you do…then you do it. If you make the decision not to do a task, then you don't do it. After all, whose body is it and where are your decisions made? Blaming others for making you do something is victim mentality and can keep you in a stuck state.

As soon as we step back and consider what the really good reasons are that we do something, it is easy to see why we sometimes do things that we don't like or want to do. As soon as we realise what the benefits are, it is amazing how much more easily we are able to complete the task. By focusing on the benefits we can move to doing the work with an attitude of acceptance. Once you accept that you do everything for your reasons not for other people's, you can easily gain momentum to move forward in your life.

The other interesting fact is that just because you get your children to do something once, strangely enough, it doesn't mean it will be any easier the next time! In fact sometimes it feels like it gets harder every time you ask them. Their resistance to doing what they don't want to do is all about wearing you down to the point where you give up and they get out of whatever it is they don't want to do. Have you ever caught yourself doing your children's chores because it is "easier to do it yourself"? What is that about?

Think about your own behaviour and consider where you use this exact same strategy or behaviour pattern, either at home or work. It is extremely empowering when we realise that we all do it! Everyone on the planet instinctively tries to do what they want to do and avoid doing what they don't want to do.

NOTES

6
LABELS MATTER

Names and labels you choose to use matter. We all know words have meaning and often use them regularly without stopping to consider their full meaning. For example, many parents use the term *pocket money* to describe the money they give their children to spend on fun things of their own choice. Consider which of the following meanings it may be possible for someone to associate with the term *pocket money:*

- It goes in your pocket so you have it with you to spend any time you feel like it.
- It is in your pocket so it's not much and doesn't matter what you spend it on.

Pocket money is a good term to use for money that you have given for them to spend on fun activities.

Another term often used is allowance. It is also worth checking on what you feel this term means, and what it means to your children. The thesaurus likens *allowance* to *payment, grant and pocket money.* You might like to consider what they are being given the money for.

We suggest you keep whatever term your family uses now for any money given to your children for entertainment, and to treat them each week and/or give them for fun. If you are currently giving them money for saving or investing, it is clearer to them if you label that money by another name e.g. *grant* or *gift for saving* and have clear rules about when (if ever) that money can be spent and on what.

When you pay your children for doing tasks around the home, that money should have a different name to differentiate the fact that they are required to work for the money. We use the term *KidsHomePay* as it reminds the children that there is a financial incentive for doing the tasks and that they are in control of how much they earn. If you would rather use a different term, discuss and decide as a family what to use. It is always preferable to use a term that has a positive meaning. Avoid using any negative labels when talking about money as it may have an unconscious negative effect in the long term.

KidsHomePay

Suggested Terminology and Meanings:

HomeTasks – used rather than *chores* as it sounds more positive.

KidsHomePay – payment for tasks completed successfully around the home or neighbourhood.

Pocket money / allowance – money given to treat your children. It is up to them as to what they spend this money on e.g. movies, food, trendy clothing items, music, etc.

Grant money – money given to your children for saving for major items e.g. investments, education fund, first car, etc. Parents should discuss with their children which is the best account to save grant money in.

Gifts – money given for special occasions or rewards e.g. birthdays, reaching goals, prizes, etc. Your children choose where to spend or save this money.

NOTES

7

KidsHomePay DAY
...REAL CONVERSATIONS
GET REAL RESULTS

When starting up the system for learning the value of money, it is important to find a time each week or fortnight to regularly sit down with your kids to discuss money and how your children are making and spending it -- call this day *KidsHomePay Day* and make it fun and important in the family schedule.

The quality of the conversation with your kids on KidsHomePay Day will determine their results in the future. Have very real conversations about the work they have done and the payment they are expecting to receive.

If you choose to pay them without checking and discussing the quality of their work, you are giving them a message about the importance of the quality of their work. What standard do you want to encourage your children to aim towards? What standard do you hold yourself accountable to? What standard do you want your children to hold themselves accountable to?

When discussing the standard to which they have completed the work, practise using language that is about the work, not them. This is achieved by separating the work from the child in the language you use to discuss it. No matter what the job they did is like, your love for them should be clearly evident to them and completely separate to the payment you make for the HomeTasks™ they do.

Discussing why the standard on work is good enough and how it needs improvement is very different to telling them they are good or bad. If you say "You did a bad job on the dishes." They may have heard "You are bad." The only way you can really know if they are hearing what you meant to say to them is to ask them to tell you back what they heard you just say. Take the time to really listen to hear what they are feeling about the feedback. Being very specific about the feedback you are giving, and offering a good reason why they should change how they did a task can also avoid confusion e.g. "Some of the dishes were not in the correct place in the cupboard. Please take care to put the dishes in the right place in the cupboard so everyone can find them easily." Give your children considered feedback that always comes from your heart.

Being honest and open about why or why not their work is to an acceptable standard, will help them become good at discerning quality in other areas of their life, and also help them improve at receiving feedback. Showing you why they deserve full payment for what they do can help them step up and own the results of their work. A great way of helping them do this is to ask them to show you what they have done. Ask them how they feel about the job they did and to rate it on a scale that describes the quality of their work. It could be fun to use ratings like superstar, professional and amateur – or better still, ask your children to come up with their own ratings. You don't have to make a huge deal of the ratings for them to learn that people who complete their work on time and to a high standard earn more money and keep their customers returning!

We do not mean for you to criticise every little detail of every job they do, rather check on a different job each week and see how they are going. It is really great if you can provide them evidence of when you have noticed they did a great job - everyone thrives on positive feedback! Focus on all of the good work they do before mentioning any areas for improvement. Ask them for suggestions on how to improve the way things are done. Then always finish your discussion with a positive comment.

> Being honest and open about why or why not their work is to an acceptable standard, will help them become good at discerning quality in other areas of their life, and also help them improve at receiving feedback.

NOTES

TEACHING KIDS ABOUT MONEY

WHAT'S IMPORTANT TO ME...

8

KIDS DO THINGS FOR THEIR REASONS NOT YOURS

We all put our resources (time, attention, money and energy) into the things we consider to be most important – the things we value most. Understanding our own behaviour is the best way to learn how to interact with our children effectively. This simple process to investigate our own values is a great place to start.

Now to do this, ask yourself the question, "What is important to me in life?" and write your answers in the space below. Write them as single words or phrases – however they pop into your mind. All of your answers are perfect for you at this time. In this quiz you always give the right answers.

Once you feel you have a complete list, ask yourself "What is important to me in life?" again. This time sit quietly and see what else comes to mind. Give yourself a couple of minutes, often the best ideas may take a while to come forward, and then add them to your list.

Once you think of all the extras that have come to mind, ask a third time and sit quietly; past your comfort zone and really check if there is anything else that is really important to you. Then add these things to the list as well. It is amazing how many people have never been asked this question, and how many are surprised by what answers pop into their minds once they are past the expected or obvious answers.

Dictionary definitions of "values" describe them as being about a person's standard of behaviour that they judge as being right, desirable or important. Values drive our lives and determine where and how we allocate our finite resources of time, energy and money. It can seem quite confusing when you try to connect your goals directly to your values because a values list will often include a mix of tangible and intangible items.

In order to further clarify what is really important to us, it is useful to sort our values into two lists. First write the abstract or intangible things you have listed in the *Intangible Values* column. Then list the things that you can see or touch physical evidence of them existing, in the second column. We use the term *Tangible Values* for these items as they are the things we are seeking to have in our lives. Here is an example of sorting Intangible Values from our Tangible Values

Intangible Values	Tangible Values
Honesty	Family
Integrity	Career
Success	Own family home
Happiness	Good Health
	Learning Golf
	Boat
	Music

In this example, family and career would end up in the Tangible Values column as they physically exist and "honesty" and "success" would be in the Intangible Values column. As you can see, our intangible values are more about how we choose to operate in the world or our human traits and behaviours.

Our tangible values are physically able to be obtained or achieved. It is the tangible values that we can focus our goal setting on and move towards achieving. When you can describe exactly what it is you want, you can set your conscious and unconscious mind in the direction of obtaining what you really want.

Now sort your list in the table below:

Intangible Values	Tangible Values

The next step in this process is to see how "real" you are being with yourself. Looking at how we live our lives and use our resources is the best way to collect evidence of whether our tangible values actually align with what we say they are.

We all have finite resources including:

- time – our most valuable resource as we can never get more of it than we have!
- money
- physical assets we own in our environment
- thoughts and problem-solving – our mental processing power
- imagination and dreams
- physical energy and effort

Next, for each question below, write your top 3 answers in the spaces. Again keep your answers to a single word or short phrase.

RESOURCES	TOP 3 TANGIBLE VALUES		
What do you spend your time awake doing?			
On what do you spend your money?			
What things have you paid for and put into your environment – at home and work?			
What tangible values do you keep physically close to you?			
What do you put the most effort and time into learning about?			
What do you think about most?			
What do you spend most of your day-dreaming time focussed on?			
What are the top things you find you do effortlessly and willingly?			
Where in your life are you most organized?			
What do you talk to other people about most?			

Once you have answered all of the questions, add up how many times each item is repeated on your list and write them in order. This will give you a list of your tangible values in order of importance to you. Compare this list with your previous list to see how closely they align.

1

2

3

4

5

6

7

This is a very important exercise to help people be realistic about what they really value and realise why they are spending their resources on specific things and perhaps not achieving things they tell others are important. Sometimes we may say things are important to us because we think that is what the person we are talking to wants to hear from us.

Once you take out the money you spend on the necessities of life, examine where you spend the rest of your money. Clearly seeing what you allocate money to and why, can help you realise how important it is to learn about your children's tangible values and what they therefore will want to spend money on.

What do you imagine your children's tangible values are? The best way to find out is to ask them. Children are less likely to talk in abstract terms so simply use the table below to fill in their answers for their tangible values.

For each question below, write your child's top 3 answers in the spaces. You will of course need to ask the questions in words suited to your children's age at the time.

Name:_____ Date/Age: _____

RESOURCES	TOP 3 TANGIBLE VALUES		
What do you spend your time awake doing?			
On what do you spend your money?			
What things have you paid for and put into your environment – at home?			
What tangible values do you keep physically close to you?			
What do you put the most effort and time into learning about?			
What do you think about most?			
What do you spend most of your dreaming time focussed on?			
What are the top things you find you do effortlessly and willingly?			
Where in your life are you most organised?			
What do you talk to other people about most?			

Once they have answered all of the questions with you, calculate how many times they mentioned each thing and help them rewrite their list in order of importance to them.

1

2

3

4

5

6

7

You will no doubt get very different answers from your children at different ages. It is really worthwhile to write your children's names and the date down when you do this exercise with them. That way you can redo the exercise each year or two and see how their values change as they age. You no doubt can remember things when you were very young that were really important to you then that are no longer important...I am sure there are some embarrassing photos in your family albums as evidence of some of the trends you lived through and identities you created for yourself in your teens and twenties! Imagine celebrating your child's 18th birthday and being able to share with all of their friends and family what they thought was really important when they were four!

Knowing and understanding your children's tangible values provides you with the opportunity to learn to communicate with your children through what they really want and create high quality family relationships.

If "having money" or a related answer doesn't come up for them, then chances are they don't understand what it really is yet and you have taken a step in the right direction to change that. If they mention buying or owning specific things, ask them what having each thing means to them to find out more about their thinking.

> Consider which of your children's answers are similar to your answers and which are similar to someone else's they have in their lives and you will also have some clues as to who else they are modelling.

What you are investigating in this exercise is you and your children's intangible and tangible values. Values drive everything we do. Have you ever noticed that as soon as your bills for living expenses become uncomfortably large, you stop spending your money on 'stuff'? It is not because you no longer want to buy things; it is more likely because you and your family's security may be under threat. You value having the security of somewhere to live and food on the table highly and therefore choose to put your money there rather than into buying a new television or other "toy".

The big question here is "How do we help our children see importance in what we consider to be important?" The answer is to help them realise how helping you get what you want, will help them get what they want! After all that's pretty much how all positive interactions work isn't it?

Parents all want their children to be safe, secure, healthy and happy. Most parents want their children to have better lives than they had growing up. They see having money as an important aspect of being able to provide this environment for their children yet many often struggle to teach their children good money management.

Some parents think 'kids should be kids' and see thinking about money as a 'bad' thing kids shouldn't have to do until they are adults. If you fall into this category, please consider where you learned about money and what the effect will be on your children if they grow up thinking it's bad to think about or focus on money.

We invite you to consider changing your own thinking by really examining it and then consider selecting new empowering thoughts around money that will be good for your children to adopt from you.

Financially secure people who don't worry about money are generally people with the mindset that it is great to think about money so you always have more than enough. It's all about what and how often you think about money. When you consider things you now do easily; you learnt the skills you have by starting with the basics and then adding new skills bit by bit to build on what you know. When you couldn't work out how to get to the next level you no doubt discovered that the best way to move forward was to go to someone who already knew i.e. an expert and find out from them. To do this you may have asked them in person, watched them demonstrate, read a book, watched a DVD or found out information on the Internet. Then you put your new understanding and information into practice...you DID it for yourself! We all then learn by trial and error... Would you rather your children make their first financial errors with small amounts of money at a young age or their first mortgage as an adult?

Take a minute to consider how you *know* that you *know* something. When asked the question, many people answer they really know something when they see and feel themselves actually doing the new thing. They also answer that they really know it in their mind. Think about what you see and feel yourself doing in the area of money and thoroughly consider if you know you are modelling the good money skills and behaviours you want for your children. Think about what your children see you do and say around money throughout the week.

A great question to ask yourself is "Who has great thoughts and actions in the area of money and how can I access their expertise to change my thinking so I become the expert for my children to model?"

Remember - You also can't teach anyone anything ...and...no one likes to be told what to do. Learning happens inside one's brain – you can't learn for them! They have to choose to learn.

As a parent you model and offer information and wisdom – your children decide whether to do what you do and to learn information you offer...or not. In their world, it's all about them!

9

KidsHomePay

The following steps outline the process for setting up a simple system for providing the opportunity for your kids to earn KidsHomePay and also for you to continue gifting an allowance to them. This KidsHomePay system can develop children's entrepreneurial skills and set them up for a life with worry free money management. They can start seeing themselves as a Business Kid and feel empowered in the knowledge that even as a young child they can have control over their finances.

The age of your children will determine how many of these steps you implement at a time and how much to adjust them to suit their stage of development. It is far more beneficial to their learning to overestimate what they can understand than to dumb it down too much and have them miss the chance to step up – it is as easy to learn to say the word *net profit* as it is to say *Grandmother*. The first time you introduce a new term to them you will obviously have to explain it to them…again, the best way for them to have real understanding of financial terms is to DO them – put them into practice everyday!

Later we will introduce you to a simple and easy way you can automate this whole process.

Step 1
Make it all about THEM – help them create a monthly Forecast or Money Plan of what THEY want

As mentioned earlier, the labels and words we use do really matter. The term *budget* is often used to describe what can feel like allocating limited income to endless expenses. To many people it evokes a similar response to the term *diet* and can feel restrictive or sound like doing without. We use the term *forecasting* as it is about creating the future you want using money to get you there.

This is a simple process of sitting down with your children and helping them do their forecast by listing all of the things they would like to be able to buy in the next week and comparing it to their income. As they get older their goals for purchasing items require larger amounts of money, so you may have to help them divide the total cost of an item by the number of weeks it will take to save for it. This will give them a realistic amount to aim for in their weekly forecast.

Forecasting helps them set a goal for how much they want to earn and makes the amount theirs to own and strive to achieve.

- Discuss what fun things they want to do with friends and family and help them work out what the activities cost.
- Ask them about things they want to buy for themselves and what costs will be involved.
- Deduct the amount you gift them as an allowance.
- They can then see how much KidsHomePay they will need to earn to buy what they want.

PLEASE NOTE: *For your convenience, blank copies of the templates used throughout the book are available for you to download free of charge. Use them as a guide to create your own or print/photocopy them for your children to use.*

Simply go to www.moneytoolkits/TKAMtemplates and download them.

Here is an example:

Rebecca's FORECAST

		Amount
THINGS TO DO	Go to the movies with friends	$9.00
THINGS TO BUY	Lunch at school	$5.00
	Pre-paid Phone	$5.00
	Play Station Game (4x10)	$10.00
	Birthday present for Dad	$15.00
WEEKLY FORECAST TOTAL		$44.00
Less ALLOWANCE	(from parents)	($25.00)
Less GIFT	(from grandparents)	($10.00)
AMOUNT TO EARN FROM COMPLETING HomeTasks		$9.00

Once they see for themselves how much they need to earn to do and buy what they desire, it is up to them to choose whether or not to do the tasks required. This is where you can help them shift their thinking about the value of the things they want compared to the things they need. If parents always give children all that they want, it will be harder for them to understand the difference between wants and important needs. Once they fully understand that it is important to allocate money to cover living expenses, they will be able to live a worry free independent life and work out how to get all of the things they want in life.

It is a great idea to have your children see themselves as a business as young as possible – the business of them! Suggest they come up with their own business name and business card so they develop their identity as a business owner. There are lots of simple to use templates in MS Publisher and Word for business cards, stationery and business forms. Help them put together a folder with dividers to file all of their business documents.

Once your children are used to this system of forecasting and you feel they are mature enough to understand the concepts involved, we suggest you introduce them to concepts of the Education and Magnet Money (Investment) accounts, whereby they contribute regularly from their earnings. Start with a low set amount of a few dollars and then introduce a percentage of their earnings to those accounts which means the amount will increase as their income increases. The idea is to work up to 10% at the earliest age possible. The next page shows an example of using flat rate contributions for Saving and Investing.

This example includes the Education and Magnet Money Accounts:

Rebecca's FORECAST for July

		Amount
THINGS TO DO	Go to the movies with friends	$9.00
THINGS TO BUY	Lunch at school	$5.00
	Pre-paid Phone	$5.00
	Play Station Game (4x$10)	$10.00
	Birthday present for Dad	$15.00
SAVINGS	Education Account	$2.00
	MAGNET Money Account	$2.00
WEEKLY FORECAST TOTAL		$48.00
Less ALLOWANCE	(from parents)	($25.00)
Less GIFT	(from grandparents)	($10.00)
AMOUNT TO EARN FROM COMPLETING HomeTasks		$13.00

In this example, Rebecca's parents have chosen to give her an extra $5.00 allowance each week provided she deposits at least $2.00 into her Education and Magnet Money accounts.

As children become used to the system, parents can choose to give children increased responsibility by increasing their allowance and increasing the number of things the child has to buy for themselves. For example once they are teenagers, you might have them manage the purchase of their own clothes so they learn how much big brand name clothing really costs before they leave home and have to manage a full living expenses budget.

Step 2
Discuss guidelines for allowances and gifts you give your children

Families have different rules about how much allowance their children receive. Some parents use $1 per week for each year of age i.e. a seven year old is given $7.00 per week. Other families use an incremental scale and have the older children manage their own purchasing of an increasing number of their essential living expenses such as clothing. This is a great way of transitioning them to living independently in the future.

We recommend you set KidsHomePay Day into the family schedule and make it the specific day that you give the children their allowance.

If they want more money than their allowance so they can buy the things they want, give them the opportunity to earn more by doing HomeTasks™. It no longer matters how much they like the task as they have their own motivation for completing it.

This is where they truly learn the value of working for what they want. Consider carefully what giving in and giving them too much today will really cost them in their future.

Once you have set up your rules around KidsHomePay and allowances, make sure you stick to them.

If your kids want to buy a more expensive item and you would like to contribute to funding it, we suggest you offer a matching program to encourage them to stay focussed on what they want. For example, if they want to save for a new bike, you might offer to match dollar for dollar what they contribute. If they play music or a sport that requires expensive, specialist equipment you may offer to contribute 3 or 4 dollars for each dollar they contribute. If the item is highly priced and you feel they should have it, consider setting a dollar figure you want them to contribute by a certain date and let them know that once they reach the target, you will put the rest of the money in to purchase that item.

Step 3
Set up age appropriate HomeTask schedules and rates of pay

Before exploring what HomeTasks™ children will be paid to complete, it may be important to discuss which tasks around the home is each person's responsibility as a member of the family. For example you may decide that everyone has to clean their own bedroom (by a certain age) and ensure all of their own things are returned to their rooms by the end of each day.

The HomeTasks™ that they can earn money for should meet certain criteria that you all agree on. These may include:

- tasks that help the whole family
- tasks that save the parents time because they work long hours
- cleaning tasks in communal areas of the house and yard
- tasks to help younger members of the family because they need help to complete some tasks e.g. vacuuming a young sibling's room.

The type of tasks that young children can complete successfully will obviously differ considerably to those of a 16 year old. The list on the following pages includes some suggestions as to which tasks may be appropriate at different stages of development. Customise the lists according to what you have observed your children are capable of completing independently. Obviously they will need some instruction and feedback to ensure they are able to complete it to an acceptable standard. It is vitally important to teach children from a young age that they should only get paid for work that is completed to a good standard.

Another consideration is what rate of pay is appropriate at the different stages of development and how physically difficult, boring, complex or messy a job may be. This is another area that parents should discuss with the children and come up with agreed pay rates. We have included some suggestions in the tables below. Again, these will vary according to your family values and income. One way to do this is to use a scale of 1 to 3 where 1 includes the easy and simple jobs, 2 includes the more complex tasks that require more effort and 3 includes the tasks that require quite adult skill levels and maturity.

Alternatively, you may prefer to reconsider all of the lower level tasks and choose to remove some from the list e.g. as your child develops it may not be suitable for them to do the simple tasks for the same money as they will do them far more quickly as their manual dexterity develops.

We also suggest you test the tasks and work out a maximum time or payment that is allowed for some tasks to be completed so that your children appreciate that time is money. It is important to help your children be efficient with their time and develop ethical work values rather than giving them the chance to take as long as they feel like to do a specific HomeTask. For example, you may choose to apply a flat rate to washing the dishes, whereas one off jobs may be better priced using time as a scale. Having kids realise how valuable time is will set them up to be aware of how they are choosing to use their time. After all, time is the only non-renewable resource – once it is passed, it is history!

The following tables provide a starting point for your family discussions. Add the extra tasks you and your kids suggest and then fill in the details to work out what the HomeTask opportunities are in your home. Have each child's resume set up and consider them to be works in progress – reviewing them a couple of times per year at KidsHomePay Day meetings will help keep kids motivated!

HOMETASK OPPORTUNITIES

AGE		HOME TASKS	Rating (1-3)	Pay rate per minute	Max Time Allowed	Flat rate	Notes
YEARS 2 TO 4	☐	Wipe up the plastic dishes	1			$0.20	
	☐	Unload cutlery from dishwasher	1			$0.10	
	☐	Help set dinner table e.g. napkins, placemats	1			$0.20	
	☐	Feed pets e.g. water and dried dog food	1			$0.20	Keep food to dried food and help clean out the bowls
YEARS 5 TO 6	☐	Take out the rubbish and recycling to the bins	1		5		
	☐	Make their bed	1		5		This may be an expected task
	☐	Clean out their lunch box	1		5	$0.20	
	☐	Dust house	1		30		Set specific areas to be done
	☐	Pack folded clothes in cupboard	1				
YEARS 7 TO 9	☐	Put dirty clothes in laundry	1				
	☐	Wipe up dishes and put away	1				
	☐	Water the garden	1	$0.10	30		
	☐	Fold own clothes	1				
	☐	Clean car interior	2				
	☐	Help wash pets	1				

AGE		HOME TASKS	Rating (1-3)	Pay rate per minute	Max Time Allowed	Flat rate	Notes
YEARS 10 TO 13	☐	Vacuuming	2				
	☐	Vacuum car	2				
	☐	Polish cutlery / silverware	1				
	☐	Clean pool e.g. vacuuming and scooping	2				
	☐	Washing — take out of dryer, fold and put away	2				
	☐	Window washing	2				
	☐	Weed garden	2				
	☐	Take garbage bins to the street	1				
	☐	Wash dog / pet	2				
	☐	Clean paths	1				
	☐	Load and unload dishwasher / wash, dry and put away dishes	2				
	☐	Clean outside house e.g. cobwebs	2				
	☐	Babysitting younger siblings	2				
	☐	Sell unwanted items on eBay	3				
	☐	Take out the rubbish and recycling to the bins	1				
	☐	Make their bed	1				
	☐	Clean out their lunch box	1				
	☐	Dust house	1				
	☐	Pack folded clothes in cupboard	1				

AGE	HOME TASKS	Rating (1-3)	Pay rate per minute	Max Time Allowed	Flat rate	Notes
YEARS 14 TO 18	☐ Word processing	3			yes	Price set per page depending on level of difficulty
	☐ Internet research	3				Rating may vary according to type of research
	☐ Set up all technology items i.e. DVD player, Wii etc	3			$5.00	To set up new DVD player
	☐ Research wanted items over Internet e.g. accommodation	3				
	☐ Babysitting	3				
	☐ Petsitting	2				
	☐ Walk pets	2				
	☐ Tutoring	2				
	☐ Reading stories to younger siblings	3				
	☐ Putting a load of washing on	2				
	☐ Wash car/boat	2				
	☐ Food shopping	3				
	☐ Prepare lunches / dinners	2				
	☐ Collect dry cleaning	2				
	☐ Clean out pantry / cupboards	3				
	☐ Iron families' clothing	3				
	☐ Clean microwave	2				
	☐ Mop kitchen floor	2				
	☐ Clean out refrigerator	3				

Step 4
Quoting for work

Work out the maximum amount you wish to allocate in the family budget to the children as *sub-contractors*. If they want to earn more than you can afford, consider which neighbours or relatives you feel it is safe for them to approach to do HomeTasks™ for. Many of the HomeTasks™ you would love completed, you can be sure other people would pay for too.

You have a fantastic opportunity to help your children really learn the basics of business by having them fill out the forms required to secure work and ensure they are paid for work completed.

Show your children how to fill out a simple quote to offer to complete HomeTasks™ for an agreed upon price. The process of quoting helps the child feel as though they are operating a business and puts more of the control in their hands.

> You have a fantastic opportunity to help your children really learn the basics of business by having them fill out the forms required to secure work and ensure they are paid for work completed.

Quoting can help teach children to find out how and when they will be paid for work they do before they commence the work. Later in life this can equate to them realising the importance of carefully checking what is in a contract or agreement and what rates of pay they are entitled to receive before they sign an employment contract.

This process of quoting for what they want to earn takes a while to set up the first time. Each KidsHomePay Day after, it will only take a couple of minutes to discuss what will be different and what will be the same based on what currently needs doing around the house.

Sample Quotation:

REBECCA'S HOMETASKS SERVICES QUOTATION						
No:	5					
Date:	6 July					
To:	Mum and Dad					
Address:	223 Happy Lane Smithsville 3372					
Day	HOMETASK SERVICE REQUIRED	Mins	Rate Per Minute	or	Flat Rate	Total
Sunday	Vacuum lounge, dining room and halls	30	$0.10			$3.00
Monday	Take clothes out of the dryer	10	$0.10			$1.00
Tuesday	Empty dishwasher and put dishes away				$0.75	$0.75
Wednesday	Take the rubbish out for collection	5	$0.10			$0.50
Thursday	Empty dishwasher and put dishes away				$0.75	$0.75
Thursday	Take clothes out of the dryer	10	$0.10			$1.00
Thursday	Clean and polish mum and dad's work shoes	10	$0.10			$1.00
Friday	Empty dishwasher and put dishes away				$0.75	$0.75
Saturday	Hose garden paths	20	$0.10			$2.00
Saturday	Put clothes in dryer - 3 loads - 5 mins each	15	$0.10			$1.50
			Amount Due			**$12.25**
Thank you for your business!						

Step 5
Work Schedule

Once the quote from your kids has been accepted, it is helpful to assist the children to create a weekly or monthly calendar of tasks. You might like to use a calendar with large squares and put it in a prominent place such as on the refrigerator.

Many busy families have calendars for all of the family and individuals' activities; simply add the HomeTasks™ to it.

Step 6
Getting paid!

Developing the habit of sending out an invoice at roughly the same time every week or fortnight for work completed is good business practice.

While your children are quite young, you will have to sit with them and help them do up their invoice. Once they make the connection between presenting you with an invoice and receiving the cash they want, your main job will be to make sure you are only paying for what you have agreed to and what has been completed to the agreed standard!

Using these methods only becomes easier when you begin to use the tools within the Money Toolkits Family Club which we will reveal later.

On the next page we have included a sample invoice from a daughter to her parents.

Sample Invoice:

REBECCA'S HOMETASKS SERVICES INVOICE						
No:	17					
Date:	21st July					
To:	Mum and Dad					
Address:	223 Happy Lane Smithsville 3372					
Day	HOMETASK SERVICE COMPLETED	Mins	Rate Per Minute	or	Flat Rate	Total
Sunday	Vacuum lounge, dining room and halls	30	$0.10			$3.00
Monday	Take clothes out of the dryer	10	$0.10			$1.00
Tuesday	Empty dishwasher and put dishes away				$0.75	$0.75
Wednesday	Take the rubbish out for collection	5	$0.10			$0.50
Thursday	Empty dishwasher and put dishes away				$0.75	$0.75
Thursday	Take clothes out of the dryer - Mum did it	10	$0.10			0
Thursday	Clean and polish mum and dad's work shoes	10	$0.10			$1.00
Friday	Empty dishwasher and put dishes away				$0.75	$0.75
Saturday	Hose garden paths	20	$0.10			$2.00
Saturday	Put clothes in dryer - 3 loads - 5 mins each	15	$0.10			$1.50
		Amount Due				**$11.25**

Total due in 2 days. Overdue accounts subject to a service charge of 1% per week.

Thank you for your business!

Once your children have developed these basic good business practices, you will be able to introduce concepts that are more complex.

Step 7
Some healthy competition

Another great strategy parents may like to use is to firstly allocate set jobs to each child in the family so they all have the opportunity to earn a basic amount of KidsHomePay each week. Then list all of the extra jobs you would like to offer as additional 'contract work' with set price and dates for completion. That way any of the children who would like to earn extra KidsHomePay have the opportunity to put in extra time and effort and be rewarded. This strategy can help children learn that there is competition in the world of business and that they can be in control of their financial results rather than merely accept a wage each pay period.

Below is a sample of how you might create a jobs list. Simply hang it in a prominent place such as on the refrigerator so everyone can see what is available and who is stepping up to earn more money. If a job is not selected by anyone, you may have to offer more money to have it completed...seems a lot like the real world, too!

Contract HomeTasks for the Week Beginning: Feb 12

Description	Payment	Due By	Contractor	Day Completed
Sweep out garage	$2.00	Sat	Kelly	Fri
Weed front garden	$5.00	Sun	?	?
Clean out fridge	$4.00	Sun	Kelly	Sat
Tidy linen cupboard	$2.00	Fri	Jill	Thurs
Wash the car	$5.00	Sat	Harrison	Sat
Vacuum the car	$3.00	Sat	Kelly	Sat
Wash and iron lounge room curtains	$10.00	Sun	Kelly	Sun

Step 8
Family Rules and Guidelines for KidsHomePay and Allowances

To check that everyone is on the same page with how things work, it is a good idea to sit down as a family and create your family rules and guidelines for KidsHomePay and Allowances. Write them down and keep them somewhere they are easy to refer to. Here are some ideas that you can use to start the family discussion.

KidsHomePay and Allowance Rules

- KidsHomePay Day is every Tuesday - after dinner we have a family meeting to discuss invoices, payments, opportunities, etc.
- On the first KidsHomePay Day of the month everyone also prepares their Profit and Loss Statement (discussed in the next chapter).
- Kids are gifted an allowance by Mum and Dad of $1.00 per week per year of age. It is paid on KidsHomePay Day.
- Mum and Dad also grant $5.00 per week for each child's Education and Money Magnet accounts i.e. $10 per week total. This amount will convert to matching the child's contribution dollar for dollar once they turn 10 years of age.
- 10% of KidsHomePay earned must be deposited in each child's Wealth Account.
- 10% of gifted Allowance must be deposited into each child's Education Account.
- Mum and Dad's KidsHomePay Tasks sheet will be posted first thing Wednesday morning for kids to nominate the tasks of their choice – first in gets their choice.
- If anyone borrows money, a promissory note is to be written up and signed by both parties and a witness. This is discussed further in Chapter 10.
- The price of certain necessities (make a list) will be paid for by parents. If children want a higher priced product, i.e. brand name product, they must save the difference in price before the purchase is made.

Family Money Forum Agenda

Given the busy lives families lead today, the weekly KidsHomePay meeting will no doubt be fairly brief!

The best way to keep kids' money learning developing is to also schedule a meeting every few months where the family spends some extended time discussing how the KidsHomePay system is working and what they could improve. Parents could also discuss one specific topic each time to help their kids develop their financial IQ.

Parents as leaders of the family, decide how formally they will manage the meetings. It would also be very empowering for the children to have them chair the meetings and perhaps lead a discussion topic.

We suggest you at least have a check list of important topics to cover each time.

The following agenda is provided to give you some ideas of how you might run a more formal meeting...remember what you pay attention to and review regularly gets learnt for life!

TIME	TOPIC FOR DISCUSSION
20 minutes	Review KidsHomePay rules ■ Are they reasonable? ■ How well are people sticking to them? Review of invoices from children ■ Are they being completed on time? ■ Are they being paid on time? Review of how well the children have completed their chores ■ are they age appropriate – are they ready to add some more challenging tasks to their list? ■ quality of work ■ how long they took ■ what would help them improve (if necessary)
10 minutes	What children did with their money / money management ■ Did they deposit into their bank accounts regularly – if not, why not? ■ Does anyone have outstanding debt (Promissory Notes) – what interest are they paying and what will that cost them in the long term?
20 minutes	Suggested Topics for Discussion – i.e. choose one to focus on at each Family Money Forum: ■ Money Rules ■ Importance of Goal Setting and Achieving ■ Money Management ■ Business / Marketing Ideas ■ Investments available
10 minutes	Questions, Sum Up and look at following week

MONEY RULES

One of the topics we suggest discussing in the Family Money Forum are your Money Rules. These are rules which your child sets for themselves and will apply to how they handle their money. They range from how you manage your money (Money Management Rules) to how you invest your money (Investment Rules). Another example might be how much interest they charge if they loan money to siblings or parents!

MONEY MANAGEMENT RULES

Most people have a particular criteria for how they invest their money (such as whether they prefer to invest in shares or property, get advice or do it themselves etc), but very few have rules for how they handle their money on a day to day basis.

Before your child starts earning an income from their KidsHomePay tasks, we suggest sitting down with them and getting them to come up with their own set of Money Management Rules, so that they know how to handle their money once it starts coming in.

Below is a list of ideas of some Money Management Rules they may wish to adopt:

- Create a money forecast for the following income period
- Stick to this forecast
- On pay day, review this forecast
- Keep receipts for all items purchased and compare them to the forecast
- Review bank statements every month
- Organise/file my bills in a folder
- "Pay Myself First" – to ensure my long term financial success
- Allocate certain amounts of money in the following areas to create balance:
  - Long term investments
  - Fun
  - Giving
  - Saving
  - Everyday living expenses
  - Education

This is explained fully in the MAGNET Money System™. For more information visit www.moneytoolkits.com

- Always look for ways to buy the item cheaper (if possible)
- Credit Cards rules (once old enough to have one):
  - Only use in extreme emergencies
  - Pay entire amount off after Interest Free Period (if applicable)
  - When it's appropriate to use and for what items

INVESTMENT RULES

Investment Rules are a more advanced concept and we recommend introducing Investment Rules after the KidsHomePay System has been used for approximately 6 months and your child's money management rules are being followed. Investment rules would include rules about:

- What type of investment to choose
- Rate of return that you consider worth the risk
- When to seek advice from a professional
- What percentage of your investments are in the different categories of risk
- Only invest in things you understand fully

NOTES

10

THE BUSINESS OF YOU AND NET PROFIT

Once your children are in the habit of earning income for themselves on a regular basis, the next really valuable concept to introduce is that of *net profit*. The earlier you introduce business concepts to your children the sooner they will be able to take the next level of wealth creation on board.

A great way to introduce basic business concepts is to help your children think of themselves as a business i.e. that they are their own business. After all, if we aren't working on *our business*, who is?

The first step is to introduce four basic business terms:

Income – any money coming in either through HomePay, wages, gifts or allowances.

Expenditure and/or expenses – any money you expend or spend on things i.e. money going out.

Profit – when you have more money coming in than you've spent, you have money left over.

Loss – when you spend more money than you have coming in, you are left owing money to someone or have to take money out of your savings.

> A great way to introduce basic business concepts is to help your children think of themselves as a business i.e. that they are their own business.

Encourage them to create a net profit at the end of each week or month. If they think of themselves as being a small business in this first stage, they will have an easier transition to working out other KidsMoneyMachines™ that don't require their time to be sold for money. This second stage in their learning is where they can really get a head start on wealth creation by starting young!

Once they are saving and investing their net profit regularly, it is only a matter of helping them learn about the ways they can invest their extra money for long term gains. By starting these habits young, you are setting your children up with resourceful habits that can serve them for the rest of their lives.

To clarify this, help your children write up a very basic Profit and Loss Statement for each pay period or month. Negotiate which time period your children would like – some people prefer to see their progress more often than others. This allows them to see first hand what income they have made, what expenses they have paid and most importantly, what net profit/loss they have created for themselves each time. As soon as they can see that they have full control over this figure, it is easy for them to see how to improve the situation.

The first level of a Profit and Loss Statement might look like the following:

REBECCA'S HOMETASKS SERVICES
Profit and Loss Statement
July 09

Income		
KidsHomePay	$49.00	
Allowance	$32.00	
Birthday Cash	$20.00	
Total Income		**$101.00**
Less Expenses		
Movies	$16.00	
Take Away Food	$20.00	
T-shirt	$15.00	
Birthday Present for Mum	$10.00	
Game Rental	$12.00	
Total Expenses		**$73.00**
Income – Expenses = Net Profit / Loss		
		$28.00

If children spend more than they have as income in the month, parents have the opportunity to have a very valuable conversation about where the extra money came from and what that means. For example if they spent money they had saved previously, how will that affect their savings goals? If they borrowed the money, when and how will it be repaid and what interest will it cost them?

These are important real life lessons that can be taught in a very real way when the opportunity presents itself. If parents simply give their children the shortfall to cover their net loss, what will that mean in the long term?

Once children are aware of what their net profit or loss is each month, the most important questions become...

- How do I manage my net profit to reach my money goals?
- How do I increase my income so I can create a higher net profit each month?

If they have chosen to borrow from someone to cover or create the net loss, we strongly recommend that you teach them to draw up a promissory note that records who borrowed what from whom and when and how it will be repaid. Consider too at what age to introduce the concept of paying interest on what they borrow – just like in the real world of borrowing money.

The best way to use this concept is to have a *Promissory Note* that is filled out and given by the person borrowing the money to the person who loans it. When you download these, you will see that we have coloured this note black and green as it is an asset to the person who holds it - black is the colour used in bookkeeping for money we *own*. The second piece of paper called a *Promissory Note Record* is a record the borrower fills out and keeps him/herself. That way they will have it in mind that they have to earn the money to pay the lender back. We have coloured the Promissory Note Record red as red is the bookkeeping standard colour for a record of debt or money we *owe*.

We have made the Note and Record the size of real money so kids can keep them in their wallet to remind them of the debt or asset each time they use their wallet.

These templates are available for free download at www.moneytoolkits.com/TKAMtempates.htm

PROMISSORY NOTE

AMOUNT BORROWED: $ _____ DATE ___ / ___ / ___

For value received, I ....

promise to pay ....
name

on or before .... / ...... / .... the sum of $........................... with annual

interest at the rate of .... per ....
signature of maker

© Money Toolkits 2011 www.moneytoolkits.com

PROMISSORY NOTE RECORD

OWE $

Money Borrowed From: ....

Amount Borrowed: $......................... Date Borrowed: ...../...../.....

Conditions: ....

Interest Rate: .... per .... Pay Back Date: ...../...../.....

OWE $

PAY BACK AMOUNT: $ _____ ☐ PAID

OWE $

© Money Toolkits 2011 www.moneytoolkits.com

PROMISSORY NOTE

AMOUNT BORROWED: $ _____ DATE ___ / ___ / ___

For value received, I ....

promise to pay ....
name

on or before .... / ...... / .... the sum of $........................... with annual

interest at the rate of .... per ....
signature of maker

© Money Toolkits 2011 www.moneytoolkits.com

PROMISSORY NOTE RECORD

OWE $

Money Borrowed From: ....

Amount Borrowed: $......................... Date Borrowed: ...../...../.....

Conditions: ....

Interest Rate: .... per .... Pay Back Date: ...../...../.....

OWE $

PAY BACK AMOUNT: $ _____ ☐ PAID

OWE $

© Money Toolkits 2011 www.moneytoolkits.com

NOTES

11

HOW TO MANAGE NET PROFIT TO REACH MONEY GOALS

...invest in the MAGNET Money® System

Once your child has started earning money and receiving their KidsHomePay, the next step is to teach them what to actually do with this money. Having your child manage their money is far more important than how much they make, as it's all about creating the right money management habits.

> With the right money management habits, they will never get into financial distress. In fact they can set themselves up with a strong foundation so that no matter how much money they choose to earn, they will easily go through life being able to do and have all the things that they want.

The MAGNET Money® system has been specifically designed to teach the fundamental principles of money management, through the importance of separating your money into different accounts for different purposes. While the main aim of money management is to become financially free, it also looks into the psychology around money and helping you shift your thinking about money to improve your results.

We all know habits are extremely powerful and make up our behaviours. Given everything in the universe has a polar opposite - you can have good habits and bad habits. Creating a positive or resourceful habit can be easy and almost automatic if you haven't already formed a non-resourceful one. Therefore, getting your child to learn supportive habits while they are young is extremely beneficial for them. The Pay Yourself First concept is just one supportive habit used within the system.

To help people really understand what Pay Yourself First means and to learn how to manage money for the long term we developed the MAGNET Money® system. The training program was developed for people aged 10 and older, though we often have people in their 40s let us know that they have used it to successfully change their thinking around money to become far more effective in their money management as adults too!

Given that time is everyone's most valuable asset, MAGNET Money® was developed as a system to use at home. For more information and to purchase the system, go to www.moneytoolkits.com.

Motivation Creates Momentum

Keeping children focussed can be challenging in our busy and complex world. Creating a Vision Board is one of the most successful and fun ways to engage children to do goal setting as it builds a high level of engagement through "creating" a future vision that inspires their action.

Help your children find and cut out pictures of things they'd like to purchase and have them paste them onto a piece of cardboard. Kids are pretty resourceful and may use magazines, catalogues, surf the net to find them or simply draw pictures of what they want.

Before pasting these pictures on their board, have your child explain to you why they want these items and what it will do for them once they've achieved them. Get them to see themselves reaching these goals. This creates more intention on your child's part and gives purpose to what they want for themselves.

Dream Gadget

As they see and feel this moment, they also believe that the goal is going to occur.

Check in with your child by asking if they feel it's really achievable and how much they want to achieve it? Ask them how it will be for them once they obtain the item they have selected. It's important to really check in with their subconscious mind as to whether it's in agreement with them achieving this goal. Get them to sit quietly for a moment and see what comes up. If they raise any objections, consider helping them revisit their goal.

Before gluing the items onto the Vision Board, ask them what it is that they want most. The thing they want most may be more expensive than some of the other things on their vision board. If this is the case it may be a good opportunity to teach them about the concept of delayed gratification. One of the biggest issues in the world today is that people want everything NOW. This has led to some of the highest debt levels and lowest savings levels in history. Saving towards a bigger goal while going without some other things that are less important will be a wonderful lesson to share with your child. Not only that, when they finally receive the thing they want most, they will appreciate all the effort it has taken to get it and value it more highly.

If they change their mind about an item they want because something better came onto the market, that's fine, they can simply paste a new picture over the previous one. If they have already started saving for the item, they can simply reallocate the money to saving for the new item.

Help them to hang it in their room where they are able to see it easily and encourage them to look at it at least twice a day. This will keep them focused on what they are working towards.

We also suggest that you help them create a Vision Board of all they want in life, not just for the things they want to buy. For example, they may wish to include a picture of your family having fun together, their friends, pets, the family camping, etc. Things that cost money are only ever one part of the complete picture of a great life!

To help children learn a more comprehensive goal setting process we developed the DESTINY Magnets Goal Setting audio. You can find out more about this fun and effective technique at www.moneytoolkits.com/shop. DESTINY Magnets is available for purchase as an audio download so you can start using it immediately.

When you start to put this into practice you will be amazed at how easy it is. Then when you access the tools in the Money Toolkits Family Club it will become even easier.

12

HOW TO INCREASE INCOME AND CREATE HIGHER NET PROFIT

... Create a KidsMoneyMachine™!!!

Once your child understands the value of money (through negotiating and being contracted to perform specific jobs around the house) and has developed great money management habits (through using the MAGNET Money® system), the next step is to increase their entrepreneurial skills by creating a KidsMoneyMachine™ that works with paying customers outside the home.

There are many businesses kids can create. Having their own Dog Walking or Car Washing business can be a great business for kids to have around the neighbourhood.

Obviously all activities should be closely supervised by parents to ensure young children are kept safe at all times.

By discussing the concept of kids owning their own KidsMoneyMachine™ with your neighbours, you can create a community of friends who support all of the kids and learn from each other. Find your neighbours who know the most about running KidsMoneyMachines™ and have them teach all of the kids – we are sure the parents will learn a thing or two from the kids down the track as well!

> **Our goal is to develop a global community that meets in person and online to connect like minded people who are proactive in learning about and developing their financial IQ.**

Go to our website and sign up for our free moneySMART$eMag to stay in touch.

A 9 year old boy (Sam) we met recently operates four businesses and earns approximately $400-500 per month. He was taught by his parents how to run a business and once he really learned the concepts and processes involved, he simply duplicated it!

There are many skill sets and concepts Sam developed which include marketing, cost of goods sold, forecasting, revenue modelling, goal setting, managing the day to day operation of running a business and many more.

He learnt to sell lemonade only when the weather is hot and to make sure he sets up in high traffic locations. Most importantly, Sam has also learned how to ask for the money; a skill most adults struggle with.

These skills are now simply part of who he is. He was excited about learning them because he generated real results with real money in real situations and can now buy real things he wants and is also investing for the really big things he wants in the future!

Allow your kids to be in control of their own future. If there's something they'd like to buy, encourage them to be creative and come up with a way to generate additional money rather than focusing on saving. Build their confidence and belief that they can achieve anything they set their minds to and remind them that it's fun to make money.

Why wait to start earning money?

NOTES

13

BORROWING AND WHAT IT CAN REALLY COST

There are no doubt occasions when your children have really wanted something before they have saved up enough money for it. Obviously the best scenario is to have them work out how to make more money so they can buy what they want sooner. Human nature being what it is; parents sometimes can't resist giving their children the shortfall required for the purchase.

This situation provides another great learning opportunity to really help your kids understand the world of money. We highly recommend that you loan your child the difference and have them draw up a promissory note to record the date, amount and repayment schedule before they buy the item! When they see what else they will have to earn or give up in order to buy the item now, they will more clearly understand what they are really getting themselves into when taking out a loan.

You may also consider whether to charge interest on the loans to teach them what happens in the real world. One of the biggest challenges for people who haven't learnt good money habits is to manage credit card debt and other loans. Helping your children really get what it means to borrow on credit is one of the most important lessons you can teach them.

This is exactly what father; Peter Davis did with his 20 year old daughter Ashlee.

"When Ashlee told me she wanted to buy an Apple iPad, we sat down together to see whether she could afford it. As she didn't have all of the money available at the time, we looked at the option of temporarily borrowing from her long term savings account" Peter explains.

For Ashlee to really understand the lesson of borrowing, they calculated what the monthly repayments would be to pay back the loan to her long term savings account. An establishment fee and an interest rate which reflected the current rate for borrowing was also included.

Once realising the repayment was $50 per week, Ashlee decided not to purchase the iPad as she wasn't prepared to give anything up (such as her entertainment expenses from her Today's Essentials Account).

Helping your children really understand what it means to borrow on credit is one of the most important lessons you can teach them. Also, learning to not borrow for the purchase of luxury items that quickly go out of fashion, can save your child large amounts of money throughout their life. Remember that borrowing is generally only good when it is used to purchase an income generating asset. Learning about this is the next level of financial IQ. The basics of this concept can also be learned through using the MAGNET Money® System. Go to www.moneytoolkits.com for full details of the system.

NOTES

14

WHEN TO HAVE AN ATM CARD vs USING CASH

As previously mentioned, nowadays the practice of paying for everything via a plastic card (i.e. ATM/key card/savings card etc.) is more convenient and commonly used. However this practice also lends itself to overspending as it is easy to lose track of what you've spent, especially if more than one person is making purchases using the same account.

Do you remember in days gone by, being paid cash in an envelope or pay packet at the end of the week? If you don't, you may remember your parents coming home and working out what money was needed to keep for essentials. Then they would have gone to the bank and physically deposited the rest of the money into their account. Nearly everything was paid for by cash. This process ensured that people saw and handled their money and were regularly made aware of how much they were earning and how much they were spending.

These days most lending institutions don't issue a key/savings card to children until they are in their mid teens. We support this requirement as we believe having the physical cash in children's hands teaches them essential life skills such as:

- Recognising what currency looks like and the different denominations
- Maths skills including addition and multiplication
- Ensuring they have received the right amount of change when making a purchase and received all of what they have paid for
- Responsibility for looking after their money
- The skill of trading goods and services for money

Most importantly, children are able to physically connect to money and place a value on how much it costs to buy what they want. There is no doubt we are all inspired more when our learning takes place in real life situations.

If you rarely keep money in your wallet and pay for everything using a card, you may have experienced the following scenario:

You know you have a $50 note in your wallet and at some point, in the future notice it is gone and believe it has disappeared or worse – been stolen. You may have found yourself asking the question "Where did that money go?" When you think back and retrace your actions, you remember exactly what you spent the $50 on and realise that it went very quickly indeed!

Doing this provides you with awareness about what you spend your money on and if you don't keep track of it, it's very easy to forget where it went and what it paid for. Would you have made this realisation if you had used your direct debit card? Probably not, you might have never fully realised that you even spent the $50.

Once your child is of the age they can qualify for a key card from the bank, we suggest encouraging them to keep to a set amount of money that they are able to withdraw each week to pay for their living expenses. We recommend helping them open the other accounts as discussed earlier to ensure they keep only money that has been allocated for spending in the account that their key card is attached to. This will not only teach them about self control and discipline, it will also teach them to live within their means.

Also, review their bank statements with them and explain to them about the bank fees and charges associated with having a key card and reiterate that another benefit of withdrawing a certain amount of money each week to live off will limit these fees. Whether they receive online or hard copy statements in the post, make reviewing these with them a regular part of your monthly family KidsHomePay meeting.

It is wise to take your children to visit your bank as soon as they are old enough to understand and well before they are eligible to use a key card to provide them with an overview of how the banking system works. Encourage them to fill out their own deposit slips and commence establishing relationships with the staff. The younger they are when they start doing banking for themselves, the sooner they will become comfortable in the banking and finance environment.

NOTES

15

CREDIT CARD vs DEBIT CARD

Credit cards, when used properly can be useful and convenient. They allow you to purchase items over the phone or online, they can be particularly useful in the case of short term financial emergencies and can even help establish a positive credit history for borrowing larger amounts of money in the future (provided they are used correctly).

The problem with credit cards is that most people don't understand they are loans and the amount you spend must be repaid with interest after the initial interest free period. So many people spend freely, forgetting this concept and get themselves into high amounts of debt that can ruin them for life, ruining their credit history and therefore their chances of obtaining credit for larger items such as car loans and home mortgages.

Credit cards also satisfy the impulse buyer in people. Impulse buying is not a great way to manage your money as buying on impulse, may lead to spending more money than you can afford and also extend your saving time to purchase the items you have planned to buy and are saving for.

Before allowing your child to apply for a credit card, ensure they can demonstrate and apply discipline and self-control. Understanding that the entire balance should be paid off every month to avoid paying interest is critical and if they know that it will not be paid off within this time, they should not purchase the item. Again, it comes back to knowledge (financial IQ), self-control and discipline.

As the purchase of many goods and services these days are made using credit cards (such as making purchases over the phone or Internet), we suggest applying for a Debit Card such as the Visa/Master Cards that are available. These cards have similar features to a credit card with one important difference – you are using your own money. It's great for online shopping and the perfect solution for all of your day-to-day financial needs. This is a convenient way to access your own money from your cheque or savings account.

Developing the habit of using a Visa/Master debit card to make particular purchases at an early age may deter your children from ever obtaining a credit card and this may also help them resist the temptation of racking up bad credit card debt.

TEACHING KIDS ABOUT MONEY

16

SHARE THE BIG PICTURE OF THE COST OF LIVING

There is no doubt your children are getting older every year – aren't we all! As they progress through their teenage years and become young adults, it is important that you take them through the family finances to help them understand the big picture of the cost of living. Once kids see for themselves what income comes into the family and what expenses go out, only then can they fully appreciate what it costs to support a family.

As you observe them becoming more confident with and knowledgeable about money, you will notice when they are ready to learn about doing more complex budgeting that covers what it means to live independently from you.

From our discussions with children and parents it appears that many families never tell their children how much money they make in their jobs. It is interesting to consider what this will mean to teenagers when they are making career choices. We strongly suggest parents show children how much people earn in a wide variety of jobs and discuss with them why the rates of pay vary so greatly. You can find standard rates of pay on government websites on the Internet. The sooner children learn that all jobs have limits to the level of salary you can earn, the sooner they will be open to learning how to run their own businesses as KidsMoneyMachines™ and have the opportunity to generate larger cashflows.

Talking with teenagers about what it means to be an adult usually generates a list of fun adult things you get to do once they come of age, such as driving a car, going out to nightclubs, going wherever they want, not having to go to school. Asking them to consider how many of these activities require them to have money to participate in them can help them realise that many fun adult things regularly cost substantial amounts of money.

Talking with your teenagers about what it means to be an independent adult (i.e. living away from home without any financial support from their parents) generates very different thinking and usually includes all of the responsibilities that go with being an adult such as going to work, paying bills, raising a family, etc. When teenagers really think this through, the link to the importance of making and managing money becomes even stronger for them.

Parents who help their children learn effective business and money making skills and habits assist them in transitioning smoothly from the dependent world of a child to the much larger and more complex world of living a successful independent adult.

NOTES

17
MAKE THE LEARNING FUN

The key to learning things more quickly and retaining information is to do it while having fun. So start playing games with your children that teach them about money. If you are already doing so, that's great. If not, there are a number of games available that help teach you about money.

Everyone at some stage or another has probably played Monopoly. If you played it when you were a child, you probably didn't realise all of the lessons that were being taught in the game.

Monopoly is a great board game to introduce your children to the basics of finance and money management. Learnings provided in this game include the following:

- beingpaidonpaydayandmakingsureyoureceiveyourcorrectpay
- receiving bonuses
- borrowing from the bank
- paying interest on mortgages
- practical maths skills
- the cost of living e.g. tax and hospital fees
- buying and selling properties
- negotiating
- location effects the value of properties
- paying rent to a property owner
- receiving rent from a tenant
- asking for the money!

If you reflect on these lessons now, you may realise that you played the game without even knowing what you were learning.

There are many other board games available that specialise in teaching kids about money ... simply search for more on the Internet and choose age appropriate games. As you play, ask your children what they have learnt about money tactics along the way,

Many money lessons learned through real life experiences can be very costly and are generally not much fun if learned the hard way. That's why games are a critical step in teaching children about money and building wealth. The best part of all about playing money games is that they have fun, which means learning comes easily.

You can also make everyday duties such as grocery shopping fun and teach your kids the value of money without having to spend money on board games. This is exactly what Carolyn did with her 10 year old daughter Amy...

Before heading to the grocery store, Carolyn and Amy set a budget and created a list of items they needed to buy. At the store, Carolyn gave Amy the responsibility to select the items, giving her a writing pad, pen and calculator to help her stay on budget and ensure they were getting good value for their money.

As most children do (thanks to the world of advertising), Amy began picking up the popular, advertised brands and so Carolyn suggested purchasing the generic brands instead and showed her how much they were saving by doing this.

Once the shopping was completed, Carolyn had Amy compare their budget to the amount they actually spent and found they had saved over $50. To put this into perspective for Amy, Carolyn then proceeded to explain that she would have to stay back at work for almost two hours at $30 per hour to make this saving. Realising this would reduce Amy's playtime with her mum, Amy quickly understood how important this saving was as spending time with her mum was very important to her.

As you can see in the story above, there are great learning opportunities for teaching kids about money whilst doing every day chores such as the grocery shopping. It is very important that kids understand the importance of budgeting and staying within their budget. Kids very rarely understand the value of money because they usually don't have to do anything to get it and often parents buy them whatever they want. Putting it into perspective for them (such as having Amy realise that her mum would have to stay back at work for another 2 hours to earn the equivalent amount to the saving they made), and making it all about them, will help them understand this more quickly. So, the next time you go shopping, don't just rush to get it done; turn the store into a real world classroom and help your kids really understand the money lesson you share with them.

NOTES

18

MONEY TOOLKITS
FAMILY CLUB

In Chapter 3, we explained our viewpoint on why managing money isn't taught in schools, because most teachers don't have the right mind set to teach your kids about money. To dedicated teachers, teaching is a calling and people who become teachers are passionate about helping kids and learning rather than creating financial prosperity.

At Money Toolkits we have spent hundreds of hours on research and development to ensure you get everything you need to help your kids get a real headstart in developing their financial savvy. The result is an amazing membership website – Money Toolkits Family Club that is packed full of the best of the best content and trainings. Have a look at it now by typing this address into your web browser http://www.moneytoolkits.com/familyclub.htm

KidsHomePay Online Tool is included in the membership and makes *putting it all into practice* simple and easy. It is a tool designed to help kids learn valuable money lessons through real life experience – every day!

There is nothing like this ANYWHERE and if you are serious about helping your kids, the easiest way to apply all the ideas we have covered in this book, is to get ONLINE. It makes it so easy for you to set up the HomeTasks that each child is going to quote for and the rest is up to the kids to manage! All of the elements of KidsHomePay covered in this book are included   in the online tool and the details are on our website.

Money Toolkits Family Club membership also includes all of the content of this book as short videos so you can review any chapter whenever you would like to recap and deepen your understanding of the principles of good money management.

There are trainings about Goal Achieving that make it a fun activity; interviews with people who have mastered money and made millions; great money saving ideas you can sign up to receive; competitions; discounts and special offers; discussion forums; webinars on current topics and much more ... we are always improving and developing the site.

The Money Toolkits Family Club is by far and away the most advanced, yet easy to use resource and when you get involved with your kids using it you will wonder why something like this didn't exist years ago.

Simply go to http://www.moneytoolkits.com/familyclub.htm and watch the short video with all the details.

At Money Toolkits we are obsessed with helping kids and young adults learn real money smarts and would love to hear any feedback or suggestions you have about what to include on the membership site.

NOTES

19

TO SUM IT UP

The responsibility to teach your children the value of money lies with you as the parent. You are in fact teaching them money values and habits from the first moment they can see and hear you.

Remember, they model you, so make sure you are demonstrating the money habits you want them to adopt. The best idea is to start before they are born and set up the two suggested bank accounts; their Education and Wealth Account. You are creating what you want for them financially well before you give them any responsibility for managing their own finances.

Children also learn from experience. It must be all about them before they become interested. Taking the time to teach them the right habits initially i.e. to manage their money correctly and to develop an entrepreneurial mindset, will provide your children with every opportunity to have a positive financial future.

If you find yourself making excuses about not having enough time to make KidsHomePay Day a regular event on your family schedule; ask yourself what things you are doing now that are LESS important than your kids having a safe and secure financial future. Cut some unimportant activities out and create time for what really matters!

If you catch yourself thinking this is too hard; ask yourself how much easier things will be in the future when you choose to help your kids develop their financial IQ now!

TEACHING KIDS ABOUT MONEY

So…

Set up the KidsHomePay system for your family and make it simple and fun…

Practice it weekly and form great habits…

And you will no doubt assist your kids before they leave home, to travel well down the path of achieving great financial results in a fun and empowering way!

To your family's financial success!

P.S.
We would love to hear all of your stories. Write to us at info@moneytoolkits.com.

NOTES

20
TEMPLATES

Templates for the all of the forms in the book are provided free of charge for you to photocopy/print or use as a guide to help your children create their own.

They include:
- Monthly Forecast
- HomeTasks Negotiation List
- HomeTask Quotation
- HomeTask Invoice
- Family Contract HomeTasks
- Profit/Loss Statement
- Promissory Note

Having the correct terms and layouts will help your children learn financial management more quickly and easily.

Simply go to www.moneytoolkits/TKAMtemplates and download them.

COPYRIGHT NOTE

Helene Kempe

Helene has worked in the education industry for 30 years and has held management positions for the majority of that time. Her leadership, management and marketing experience coupled with her teaching and learning in the creative and visual arts, provides her with a valuable skill set for "thinking outside the square".

Helene holds a number of qualifications including a Graduate Diploma in Educational Administration, Diploma of Teaching, Diploma of Visual Arts, Master Neuro-linguistic Programming and Results Coach, Associated Certified Meta-Coach (ACMC) and Demartini Method Facilitator.

One of Helene's passions is to help people create their own personal power through gaining the understanding that they own their own learning and that when they focus on what they really want in life, they can achieve it more quickly and easily.

Nicole Clemow

Nicole has always had a passion for finance. After completing her Bachelor of Business (Accounting) degree and Advanced Diploma in Financial Planning, she worked in the financial planning industry for over 8 years. Her roles included working as a Paraplanner, Technical Manager and Financial Planner.

After discovering that many people had very little knowledge in money management, Nicole decided to leave the corporate world and venture out on her own to help change people's thinking around money. She has completed a Master Level in Neuro-linguistic Programming and Results Coaching and uses these effective personal development strategies learned through her study, on a daily basis.

Nicole believes that personal development is extremely important and has travelled across Australia, Canada and the USA to work with some of the top people in the field of wealth creation and financial management.

Money Toolkits®
Nicole and Helene are co-founders of the company Money Toolkits®
which was established to:

Create positive generational change
by helping families improve their Financial IQ basics.

Please send any questions or feedback to:
info@moneytoolkits.com

CONTACT US

Helene Kempe
Nicole Clemow
Money Toolkits®
www.moneytoolkits.com
info@moneytoolkits.com

CPSIA information can be obtained at www.ICGtesting.com
Printed in the USA
LVOW12s1954300414

383894LV00031B/1625/P